Sofie

and Good Manners

For parents, grandparents, teachers, nannies, and **children**

Yelina Nieto   *Lucía Guzmán*

2020

ISBN: 978-1-7336489-2-9 (ebook)

ISBN: 978-1-7336489-6-7 (paperback)

We dedicate this book to

every child in the world,

especially our grandchildren

    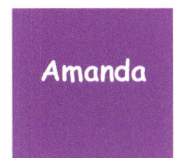

3

We would like to thank our families for their support, Sofie's parents for their collaboration in this book, and the dear friends who - Thanks to their many years in the field of teaching – gave a special touch to this publication: Terry Ellis and Miriam Bley.

Prologue

In this book you will find a practical way to teach your children the main points of good education and good manners. The sooner you start, the better the result will be for your children, caregivers, parents, and other surrounding people. The best way to use this book with small children, is to read one page every day and make comments. Allow them time to look at the pictures and to ask questions about them. If you are a teacher, you can do the same with your students in your class.

As parents, you are going through the great adventure of educating your greatest treasure: your children. For us, our little ones are princes and princesses, and like any royalty, they should receive a good education to know how to behave in life. They must be taught that their actions come along with great or not so great results. Encourage them to do at least one good action daily. Remember that the best education for them comes from the adults being their best role models.

The pictures in this book will make it more entertaining to read.

"Practice empathy and treat others as you would like to be treated."

Our character is called
Sofie

Sofie is a beautiful girl. She will show us the main elements about good manners.

We hope this book turns out to be a useful tool to encourage the children to behave properly and show good education.

Through the book, we will navigate through behaviors such as being grateful, sharing, practicing table manners, and learning what is expected from them in sacred places. In other words, to live in harmony with their family and people around them.

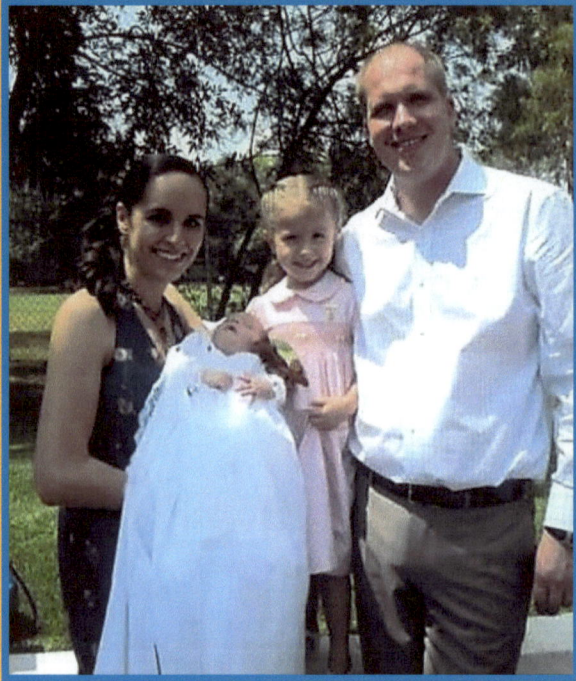

Sofie knows that there are rules she should comply when she is around family and friends, when outside home, at school, and elsewhere.

These rules have been taught to her gradually by her parents and teachers.

Sofie likes

Taking care of her belongings

Going to the zoo

Practicing sports

Listening to music

Saving

Being generous

Reading

Painting and drawing in the places where she is allowed

Sofie loves to wear costumes

During Carnival and costume parties

When she plays with her friends

For plays in her school

Otherwise, she dresses according to the occasion.

If she is invited to a pool or beach party, she wears something on the top of her swimsuit until she gets there.

Sofie enjoys going out

She enjoys her outings

She follows the rules

She stays nearby the adults

She uses the sidewalk

She does not listen to intruders

She uses a proper tone of voice

Neither does she accept presents of any kind from strangers

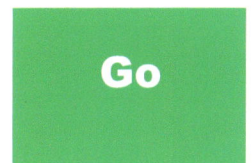

Stop

Think

Go

Sofie visits somebody else's place

She knows how to behave

She is very respectful

She uses the magic words *Please* and *Thank you*

She adapts to the rules of the place where she is visiting

Sofie and the germs

She knows about germs and hygiene

She also knows about the consequences and illnesses related to the lack of hygiene

She washes her hands before eating, after playing outside, or on the floor

She discards any food that she finds on the floor

She goes to bed wearing clean pajamas on her clean sheets

Sofie

behaves like a princess and uses the *Magic Words* since she was a baby

Good morning!
Good afternoon!
Good night!

She always remembers to say: **Please!** *Excuse me!* **Thank you!**

She answers: *You are welcome*, when someone thanks her.

She apologizes when needed.

Sofie says: *Thank you!*

- When she gets a present
- When somebody does her a favor
- When someone helps her
- When she gets an invitation
- When she leaves a party

Thank you!

"Gratitude is not only the greatest of virtues but the parent of all others." Cicero

Sofie greets and smiles her parents, caregivers, siblings, and others:

- when she wakes up

- who live with her

- when she arrives from school

- when guests come over to visit

- when her parents come back home from work

"A warm smile is the universal language of kindness." William A. Ward

Sofie apologizes

✓ When she bumps into someone

✓ When she makes a mistake

✓ When she is not on time

✓ When she damages or breaks something

✓ When she mistreats someone

✓ When she does not do what was expected from her

✓ When she wets someone - unintentionally – with her soap bubbles

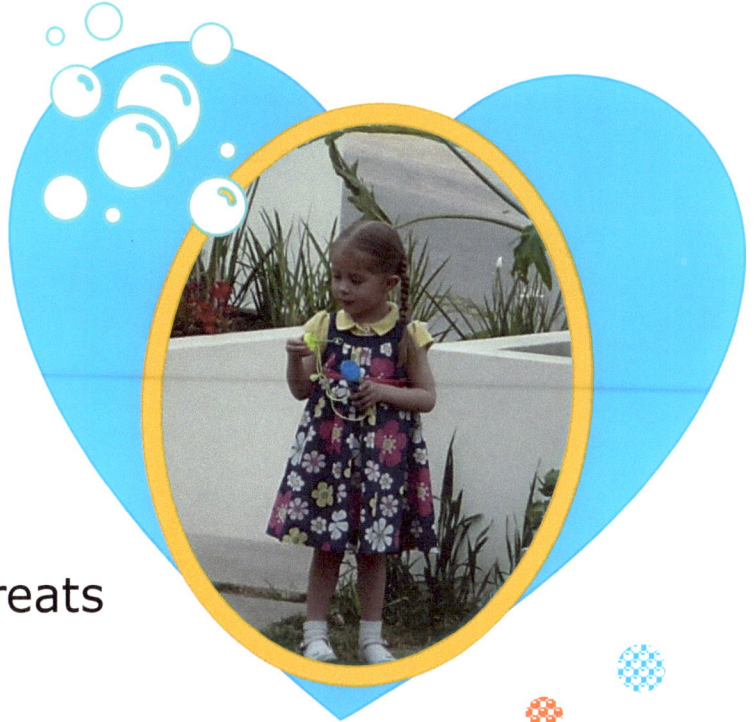

It is never too late to apologize.

Sofie and her table manners

Bon appetit!

She is learning to use the spoon - the fork - and the knife

Uses her napkin to wipe her mouth

She tries to sample all the food being served

She is learning to share - whatever is on the table - is for all of those present to eat. When she finishes her meal, she asks to be excused.

Start

Pause

Finished

or

Sofie understands the value of being responsible at home

It is rewarding and fun to be able to set a table.

✓ There is a place for everything that we need to use on the table

✓ The knife and the spoon go on the right side of the plate

✓ The fork goes on the left side

✓ The glass goes on the right side by the knife

✓ The napkin goes next to the fork

When she sits, she takes the napkin and place it on her lap. She is learning the difference between finger food and the food to be eaten using her knife, fork, and spoon.

Note

to parent and teachers: The children and you can prepare an arts and craft activity by drawing a placemat that shows the correct place for everything.

Sofie is learning that when she seats at the table she should avoid:

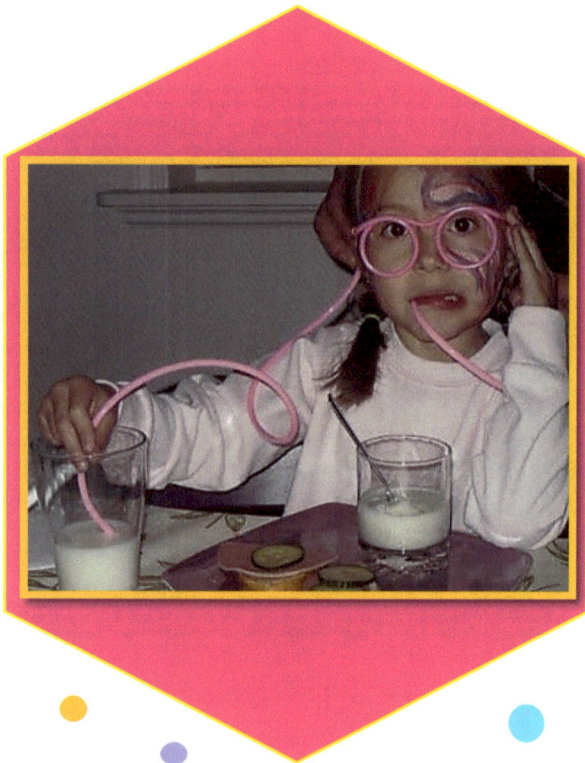

- Playing with the food
- Making noises with the food
- Placing her elbows on the table
- Chewing with her mouth open
- Eating too close to her plate
- Playing with electronic devices
- Talking with the food in her mouth

Incorrect "no oars"

Once a fork or a knife has touched food, the utensil does not touch the tablecloth again.

In a restaurant and at her table at home

She practices her table manners

She remains seated

She talks with her company

She does not play - except in the indicated places - if they are available

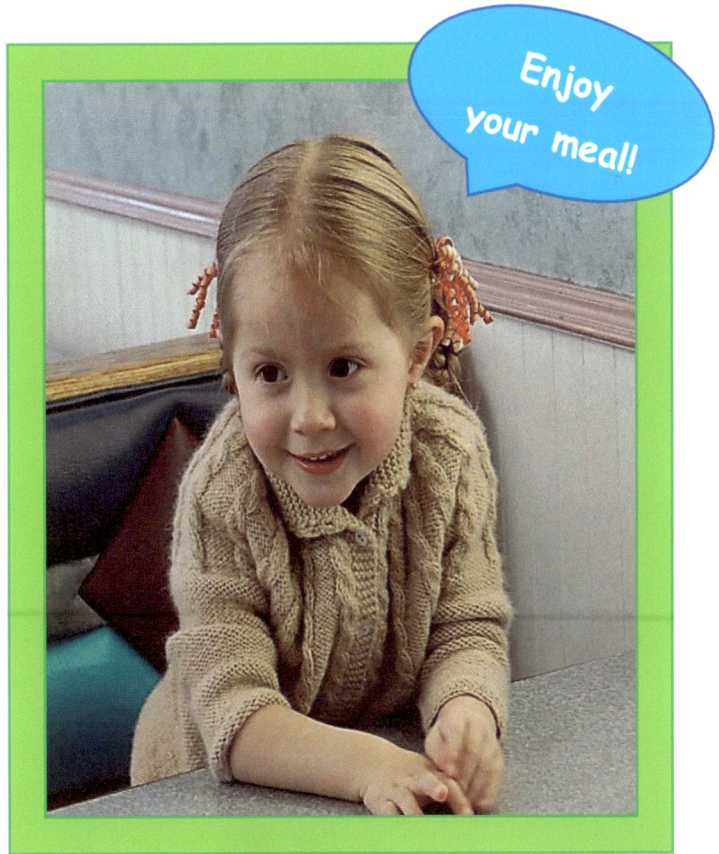

She eats what she served herself, until she feels satisfied. If she is not sure that she will like what she selected, she takes a small amount.

Enjoy your meal!

Sofie also knows that there are more things that she should avoid at the table such as...

- Criticizing the food
- Brushing her hair
- Sleeping
- Reading or coloring
- Feeding the pets
- Rocking the chair
- Playing with silverware – napkins – or plates
- Leaving it before being excused to go

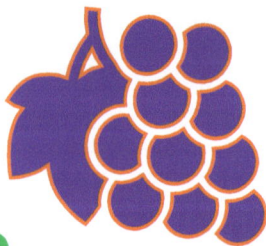

Note

At the dinner table do not:

- Blow on your food
- Make funny noises
- Take your shoes off
- Blow your nose or burp
- Lick your fingers

Sofie practices table talk

Talks politely with other people at the table about her day and her interests

Uses an appropriate tone of voice

Waits for her turn to speak

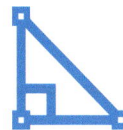

These figures will give you ideas for table topics.

Sofie after finishing

Places her silverware on the plate

Wipes her mouth with her napkin, and places it on the table

Offers help to clean up after the meal

She thanks for the meal

Note

After finishing eating, the cutlery is placed on the plate, as in the photo. The napkin is left without folding. ❀

If you want to compliment the food, you can say: "What a fantastic meal!"

Sofie knows that, since everybody is done at the table... She is free to go to play and color with her crayons.

What is your favorite color?

Serendipity

One day Bea, Sofie´s mother, said: Sofie, I am thoughtful, because we have to move to another place.

Sofie answered: Mom, do not worry. In our new address, I can make new friends.

Bea felt more at ease and smiled at Sofie's answer

Sofie goes to school

Respect and pays attention

She raises her hand if she needs something

She treats everybody with respect

She throws the waste in the trash can

123

ABC

During recess, she plays with her classmates

Once she gets home, she does her homework and shares with her family what she has learned.

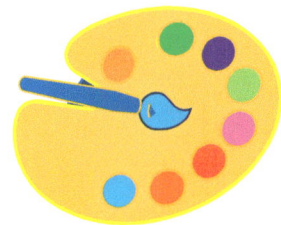

Sofie helps at home

Helping with the housework

Setting the table

Playing with her brother, Andreas

Cleaning up her toys

Making her bed

Watering the plants

Throwing out the trash

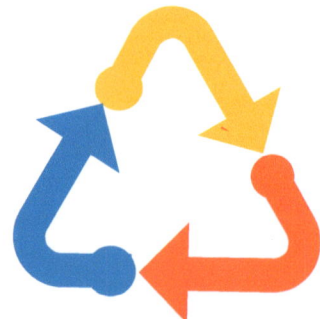

28

Sofie takes precautions

knows that she may not open the door to strangers or give information on the phone

knows the complete names, address, and phone numbers of her parents

knows the dangers of playing with fire

Only goes in the pool when an adult is watching. Uses floaties at the pool and at the beach, until she learns how to swim well.

Sofie plays with her brother and friends

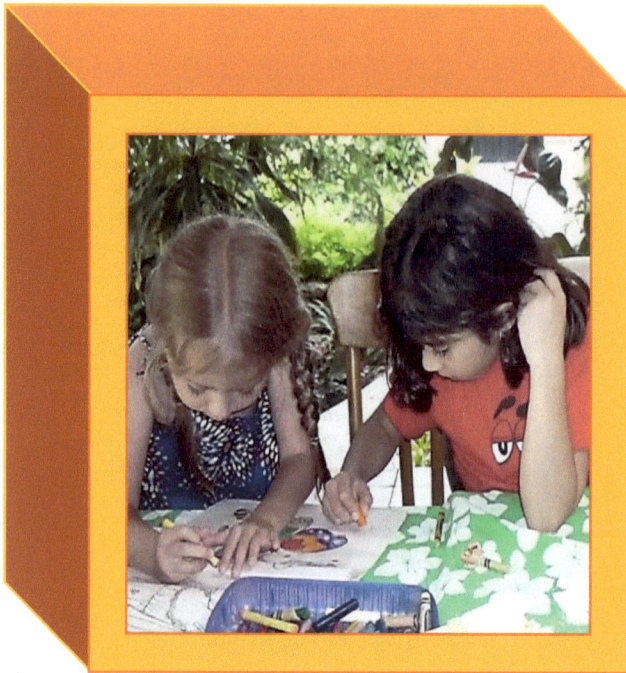

- Share the space and the toys
- Respects other's belonging
- Plays by the rules
- Keeps her hands to herself
- Uses an appropiate tone of voice
- Cleans up after finishing

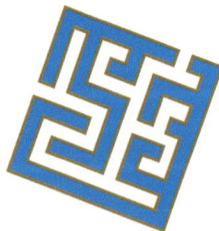

Sofie appreciates art and...

She likes to go with her family to:

- The circus
- The theater
- Museums
- Art exhibitions
- Movies
- Concerts and musicals
- Dances like ballet, jazz, and folklore

Sofie in the park

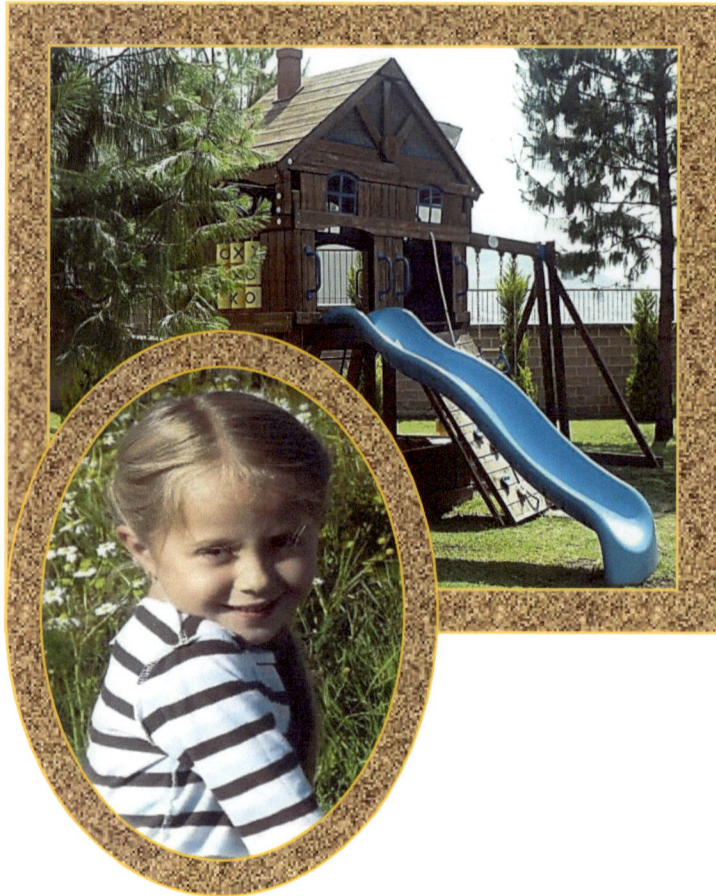

First, she **carefully** observes how to use the different attractions of playground before using them

Takes good care of the park

Plays with friends

Enjoys the playground

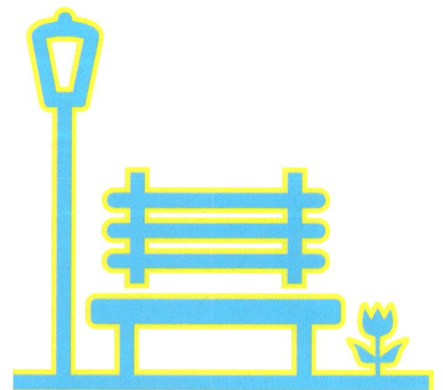

She does not feed or disturb wild animals.

Sofie is very careful and follows rules... such as:

🕐 Respects schedules at home and is learning to be punctual

👨‍🍳 Follows the directions in the recipes

Wears a seat belt in the car

✂️ Puts things in their place after wearing them

🚪 Knocks on the door before entering

🥿 Wears slippers at home

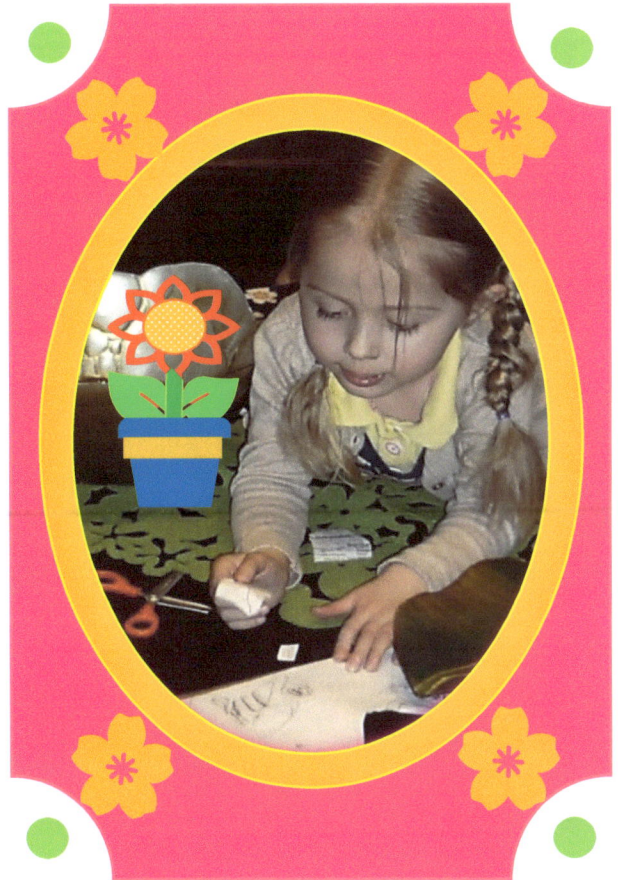

If she needs something that is not hers - she borrows it - and she returns it in the equal or better condition.

Sofie in her bedroom

Sofie likes the organization and order in her house

She enjoys keeping her things in their right place

She hangs her clean clothes in the closet

She uses a basket for the dirty clothes

She turns off electronic devices and lights in use

She makes her bed now, although when she was younger, her mother would help her out. Now - that she is growing - she does it all by herself.

She respects "quiet times."

Sofie and her hygiene

Washes her face when she wakes up and brushes her teeth

Washes her hands when she gets home and before she eats

Brushes her teeth after every meal

Blows her nose and cleans it with a handkerchief

Covers her mouth when coughing and sneezing

Sofie in the bathroom

She does not share details of her needs to visit the bathroom. If she needs help, then she whispers it to her mom.

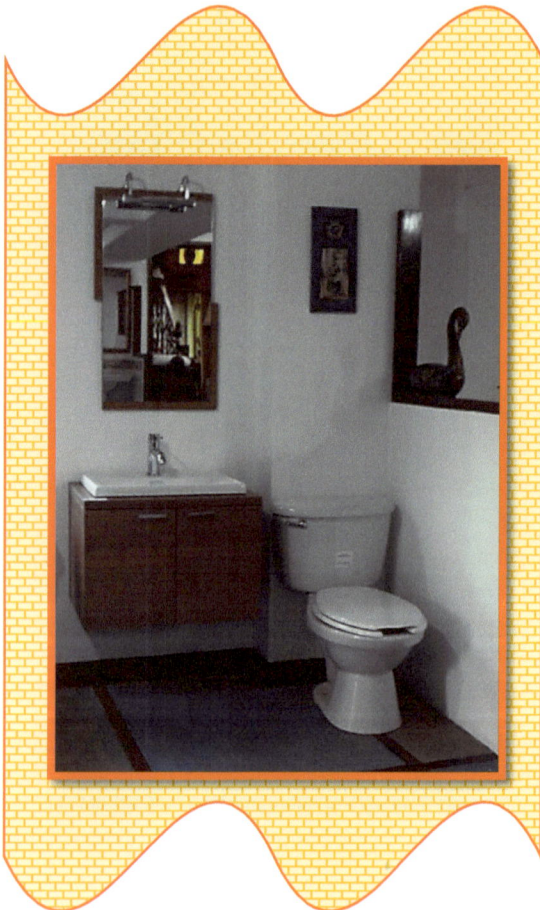

She uses the toilet paper wisely

She flushes the toilet

She washes her hands, and dries them with the hand towel

She does not leave the water running if wasted

She leaves the place nice and clean

Paper roll instruction: If you empty you replace it.

Sofie and bathtime

She knows about:

Getting her hair and body wet

Washing her hair

Cleansing her body with soap

Using shampoo and conditioner

Rising the soap

Cleaning her ears

Note

You can clean your eyes, nose, teeth, and ears in the bathroom.

Sofie and her hairstyle

Sofie enjoys wearing many different hairstyles.

Sofie's classmate - Luisa – asked her mother – Ana – to call Sofie's mom, Bea.

When she did, she told Beatriz that her daugther really admires the hairstyles that Sofie wears to school.

Then Bea and Ana made a plan to get together, so Ana could learn how to style Luisa's hair.

It is fun to share what you enjoy with your friends.

Sofie in her play area

She keeps it tidy

She uses her toys respecfully

Once she has finished playing, she puts everything back in its place

Sofie listens and obeys

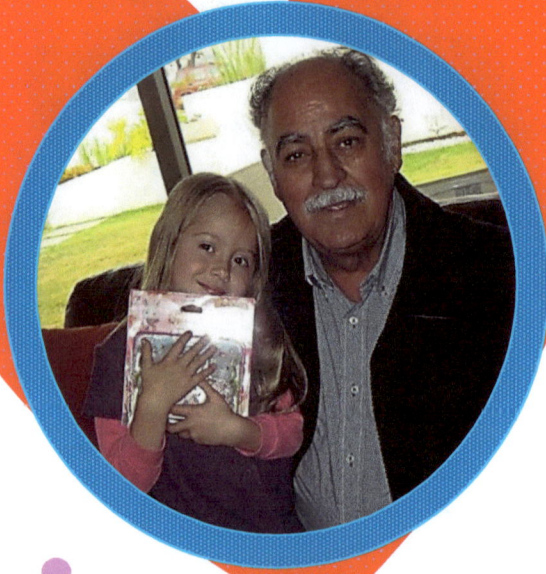

- ♥ Mom and dad
- ♥ Grandparents
- ♥ Uncles and aunts
- ♥ Older brothers and sisters
- ♥ Teacher
- ♥ Babysitters
- ♡ Caretakers

Sofie respects and is very patient with ederly people.

Sofie knows that the world is big

- She knows about different cultures, languages and climates

- She eats different typical foods

She speaks Spanish with her mom, Norwegian with her dad, and English at school.

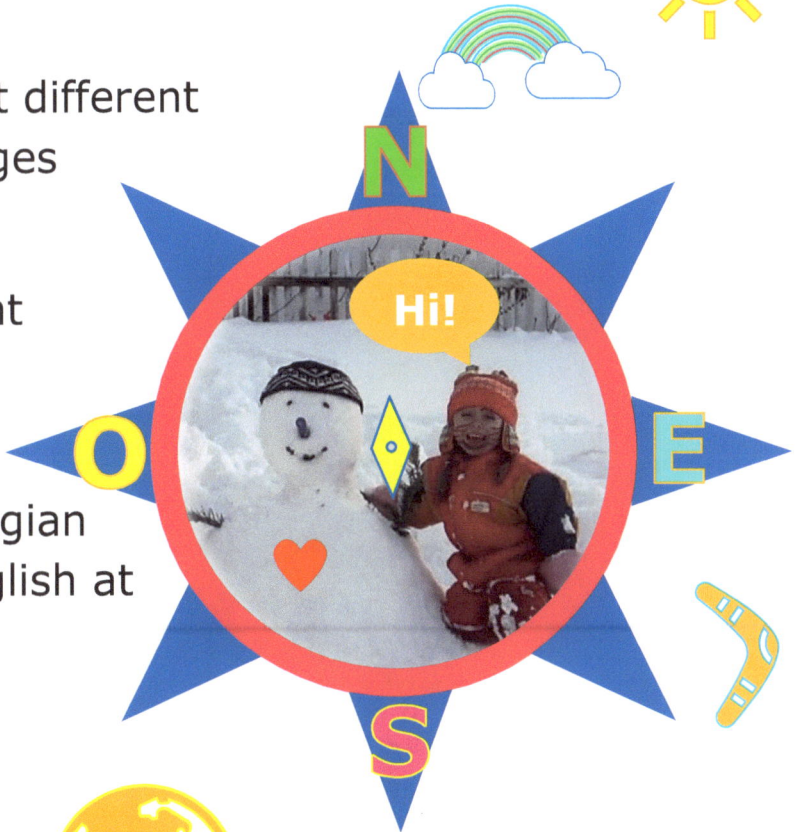

Hi!

Hallo!

¡Hola!

Sofie in the church, temple or synagogue

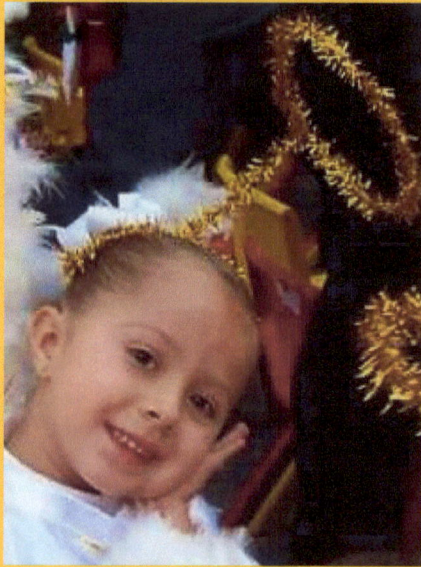

Pays respect to the priest, pastor or rabbi

Listens to the ceremony

Knows that it is not a place to play, eat or sleep

Respects the sacred places of her religion and those of others

Sofie loves her country

The music of her country and its traditions

The history

The food

The people

She respects the rules

She keeps the streets and parks clean by putting the trash in the right place

She has visited different places in her country from a very young age

"Nobody loves his country because it is great, but because it is his." Seneca

Sofie knows that there are words and gestures that she should not use:

Such as sticking her tongue out

Saying bad words

Being rude and unkind

Answering with a bad attitude

Sofie knows that there are proper ways to ask for something politely. If her parents can not get it, she accepts this. She understands that she can not always get what she wants.

The law of the boomerang - cause and effect - says that the good or bad we do, it will be returned to us.

Sofie loves Mother Nature

She takes care of the plants and flowers

She uses water wisely

She loves animals

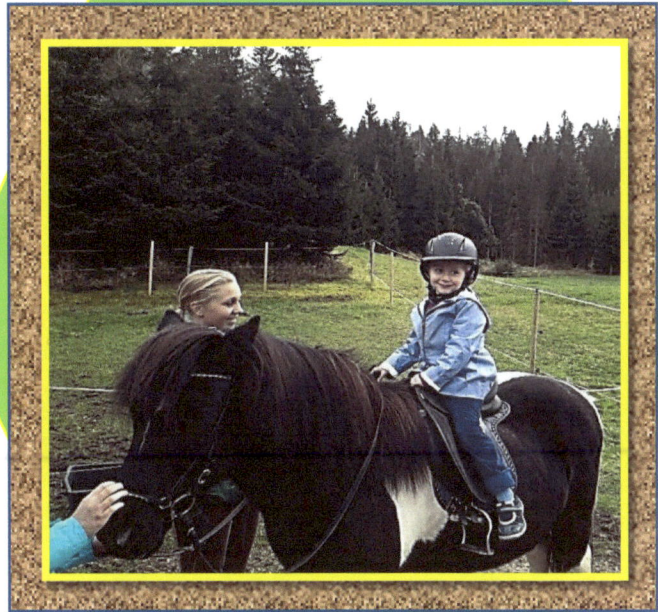

She puts the trash in the right places, whether she is outside or at home.

Sofie knows that recycling is important.

Sofie says NO

No!

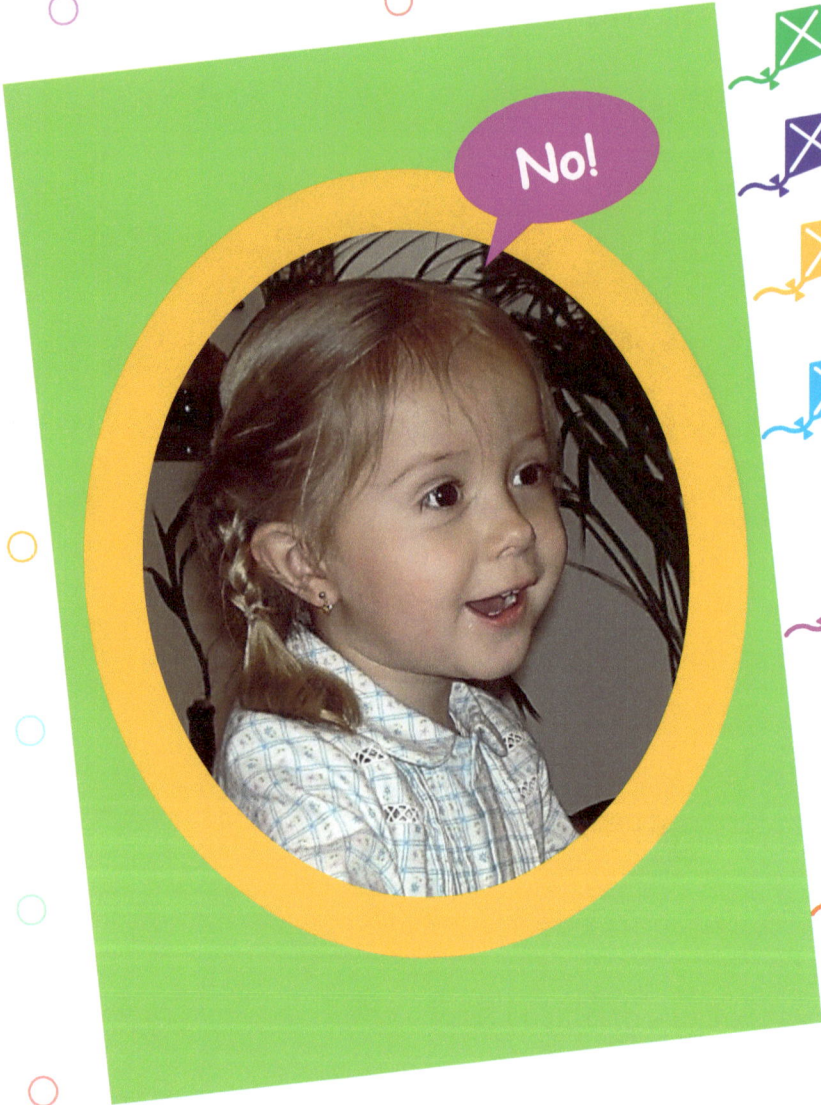

- To disobeying
- To lying
- To bullying
- To hurting feelings
- To taking things that do not belong to her
- To cigarettes and any other unhealthy habits
- She does not stay near people who are smoking

Sofie treats everyone very politely

- She speaks up when someone is not fair

- She excuses herself if she needs to

- She uses her magic words

- She speaks kindly

- She is fair

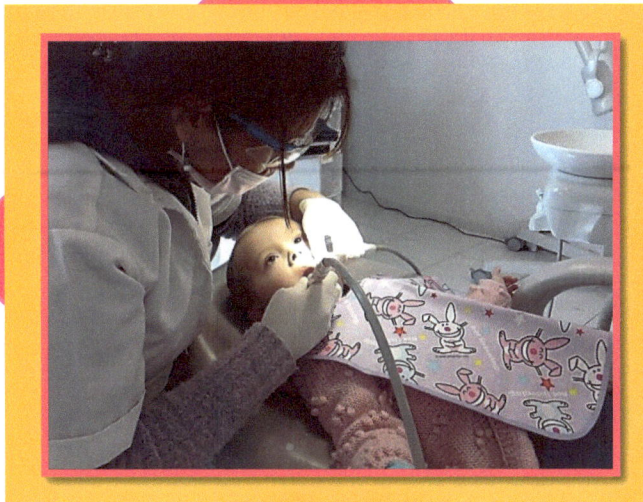

- She asks for an adult's help if it is necessary

- She is good at the doctor or dentist's office

Sofie and electronic devices

Sofie prefers to enjoy nature with her brother, family and friends, rather than playing with electronic devices or watching TV.

When she uses the cell phone, the computer or the tablet, she knows that there are set time limits and rules for them.

Sofie knows that she should treat people online with the same manners she would use in person.

She always leaves her tablet at home when she goes to a party or visits a friend.

She has learned that smiling, sharing, respecting, and helping out is an excellent way to get along with family and friends.

...last but not least, Sofie shares with you some advice:

"Practice good manners always and everywhere. Remember that if we are well-behaved, we will always be welcomed."

From birth to 12 years

Newborn: talk, sing, and smile to your baby. They are already learning from you and their surroundings. Always be nice to them. Babies are like sponges; therefore, they are always absorbing. You are educating them since day one.

6 to 12 months: They are beginning to speak. Keep modeling the use of Magic Words such as: Thank you! please! Help them to drink out of a training cup. They will start eating finger food.

1 to 1 ½ years: Model good manners and sharing, and they will try to imitate. They can understand short instructions, they begin to eat by themselves, always offer them an appropriate spoon. Teach them to greet others. Offer them a napkin.

1 ½ to 3 years: Kindness and the tone of voice can be heard and felt by a child, so make sure you use the right tone at home, so the children imitate when they are out. During mealtimes, you can offer them an appropriate fork and a zippy cup for drinks.

3 years: Do not lose your patience and do not forget your manners. Remember that they will imitate you. They eat by themselves. They are toilet trained. Teach them to tell you privately if they are going to do number one or number two, letting you will know if they will need help. Emphasize the use of good manners.

4 years: They can get dressed by themselves. Teach them to choose the clothes depending on the occasion and the weather.

5 to 8 years: Ask them to help set the table. Teach them to thank in a written form with homemade cards. Remind them to behave before going out.

9 to 12 years: They have internalized rules and good manners. The want to be successful and, if they practice good manners, everything will be easier.

Tips to reinforce manners

✓ If you have a special occasion, make sure you have everything you need for what you have planned to use. Suggest them to decorate the table with flowers and place the names of your guests.

✓ Pretend a formal dinner with special guests. Dress them up and let them practice all what they have learned and seen about manners and etiquette. Set the table, decorate it, let them write down the names of the guests, place dishes, silverware, glasses, napkin, etc.

✓ When you have guests for Thanksgiving and during Holiday celebrations, or hosting a friends and family reunion, let them use their imagination for decorating and entertaining.

✓ Plan a short play with them.

✓ Use different props and puppets, which they can include as part of their show, as they seek to illustrate the good use of manners. This is great.

✓ Kindness and good manners should be part of our daily routine and not only when there are guests at home. Please, thank you, good morning, good night, and excuse me, should always be used.

✓ Make your children notice when you are out and about and when they are watching TV, the lack of manners showcased, and they will learn that this is not a good thing to imitate.

✓ You can have a slogan at home: "Small details make great differences". Practice and you will see.

Rules at home

✓ _____

✓ _____

✓ _____

✓ _____

✓ _____

✓ _____

✓ _____

✓ _____

✓ _____

✓ _____

✓ _____

✓ _____

✓ _____

The authors

Yelina Nieto Guarirapa

This Venezuelan writer is a multifaceted person who has much to contribute to the new generations. Her passion is to travel, which she has done since she was young and has lived in several places. She graduated with a High School degree from the Teresian College in her hometown of Caracas. She earned her Degree in Civil Engineering in Worcester, MA, United States. In addition, she has received diplomas in Protocol, Finance, History of religions, and in several other courses in different topics such as: Etiquette for Children, Psychology, Coaching, Reiki, among others. As a mother and grandmother, Yelina Nieto has many suggestions that can help us parents, in raising our children. The knowledge that the writer has acquired, can be seen in her books: **The Protocol and Etiquette for Successful Couples**; **Un Hogar en Armonía**; **El Protocolo y la Etiqueta de una Pareja Exitosa**; **La Convivencia en Armonía** (Second Edition); **Más de 100 ciudades visitadas y más de 10 ciudades vividas**; **El ABC de la Buena Educación**; **Hagamos de una casa, un Hogar**; **La Convivencia en Armonía** (First Edition).

She is a great motivator. She has given courses, workshops, and conferences in schools, universities, and companies, always transmitting to those present, the desire to succeed in life.

Lucía Guzmán Bello

Lucía Guzmán Bello is a Venezuelan educator, graduated from Saint Lawrence College in Kingston, Ontario, Canada, in 1982. Since then, she has influenced the lives of hundreds of children and teachers of different nationalities. Before studying education, she had obtained a degree as an Administrator of Tourism Enterprises at the Institute of New Professions in Caracas, Venezuela, and while working this profession, she developed her passion for traveling around the world, and learning more about it.

Lucia obtained her High School degree from the Teresian College, in Caracas, where she was a fellow of studies of Yelina Nieto.

Since 1982 she never stopped her practice as an educator, currently praising education by providing individual tutoring. In her free time, she enjoys visiting her daughters and grandchildren: Marcela Alejandra and Pablo Alejandro. Always keeping the desire to continue exploring the world.

Here we leave this beautiful book that is full of ideas, photos, and suggestions that the family - especially - the younger ones will love. The best gift a person can receive is knowledge to help him or her succeed in life. In addition to entertaining, children will learn that their good behavior will make them more enthusiastically received wherever they go.

If you have any comments or questions, please contact the authors.

Their electronic mails are:

abiylosbuenosmodales@gmail.com

luciaguzman17@hotmail.com